THE OLD SOUTH

THE OLD SOUTH
50 ESSENTIAL BOOKS

Clyde N. Wilson

SOUTHERN READER'S GUIDE

SHOTWELL PUBLISHING
Columbia, SC

THE OLD SOUTH: 50 ESSENTIAL BOOKS
Copyright © 2018 by Clyde N. Wilson

ALL RIGHTS RESERVED. No part of this publication may be reproduced, distributed, or transmitted in any form or by any means, including photocopying, recording, or other electronic or mechanical methods, or by any information storage and retrieval system without the prior written permission of the publisher, except in the case of very brief quotations embodied in critical reviews and certain other non-commercial uses permitted by copyright law.

Produced in the Republic of South Carolina by

Shotwell Publishing, LLC
Post Office Box 2592
Columbia, South Carolina 29202

www.ShotwellPublishing.com

Cover Image:
Cover Design: Hazel's Dream | Boo Jackson TCB

ISBN-13: 978-1947660069
ISBN 10: 1947660063

10 9 8 7 6 5 4 3 2 1

For Paul Graham

Peerless Comrade-in-Arms

So face with calm that heritage/And earn contempt before the age. —Allen Tate

The South is a garden. It has been worn out by the War, Reconstruction, the Period of Desolation, the Depression and the worst ravages of all—Modernity; yet, a worn-out garden, its contours perceived by keen eyes, the fruitfulness of its past stored in memory, can be over time, a time which will last no longer than those of us who initially set our minds to the task, restored, to once again produce, for the time appointed unto it, the fruits which nurture the human spirit and which foreshadow the Garden of which there will be no end. —Dr. Robert M. Peters of Louisiana

Preface

THIS IS A READER'S GUIDE for Southerners, for our numerous friends from other climes, and for honest seekers of the truth of a subject that looms large in American history and culture. I have avoided recommending the works of hostile outsider criticism, which are vast, redundant, and are inaccurately reported in highly respectable circles to be definitive. For the most part I have allowed the South to speak for itself through its own large, unique, and admirable writing.

Should this work prove to be useful, the Lord willing, and the Saluda river don't rise too high in the Dutch Fork, it will be followed by reader's guides to the South in War and Reconstruction and the New South.

The selections are about equally divided between history and literature, with an occasional work of another kind. Good historians are aware that the best creative artists, fiction writers, and yes, even poets, convey understandings of human experience that the historian's supposed factuality cannot offer. This is true despite the fact that the shelves are groaning with vast quantities of bad historical fiction—the bad writers usually being the most popular. ("John Jakes and Alex Haley, call your office!") The South's voice has nowhere been stronger and truer than its great creative writers, who are indeed a marvel of the world and perhaps the high point of American culture.

History is not a science but a literary exercise in reconstructing the human past in a way that is supported by evidence. There are very few final answers in the study of history because there are always different perspectives on the same experience. Good historians know that however conscientiously they try to control their own personal perspective and the inescapable matrix of their own time, there is no perfect objectivity. History is a story and a story has to be somebody's story.

I have not tried to trace the different editions and publishing history of the books. I am aware of the value of the bibliographer's art, even rather practiced in it, but it would introduce unnecessary clutter into the simple purposes of this book that would be of little use to the reader.

Likewise, I have not said anything about how to acquire particular books. Most serious readers are these days able to access the large number of older works that are available in electronic format, often for free. Further, college and public libraries have for several decades now been zealously discarding good older books in order to convert themselves into politically correct multicultural Media Centers full of electronic texts and nonbooks. A good side effect of this evil and stupid campaign has been to make a vast number of good books available on the used book market at modest prices.

The idea of this book was in part inspired by my collaboration with my esteemed friend Howard Ray White in establishing a website for the Society of Independent Southern Historians. That site (southernhistorians.org) is a reader's guide to Southern history and culture far more exhaustive than is presented here.

Clyde N. Wilson
Dutch Fork, Republic of South Carolina

1.
At the Moon's Inn by Andrew Lytle

THIS IMAGINATIVE RENDERING of Hernando DeSoto's heroic exploration during 1539-1542 of what was to become the South is an important piece of what might be called pre-Southern history. The South does not yet exist, but its reality is anticipated by an author who is one of the great figures of the 20th century Southern Literary Renascence and who has written some of the most profound works about our region.

Andrew Nelson Lytle (1902--1995) was a native of Middle Tennessee and an unrepentant participant in the Vanderbilt Agrarian cause. He spent some time on the Broadway stage and as a hands-on agrarian before becoming editor of the *Sewanee Review* at the University of the South, which under his direction gained international reputation for its fiction, poetry, and criticism. "Mr. Lytle" until his last days was famous as a host and raconteur at his log house at Monteagle, Tennessee, where he was visited by and inspired countless writers and teachers. To pursue his writings further one should look at his *Stories: Alchemy and Others;* his Old South novel, *The Long Night;* and his essays in *From Eden to Babylon.*

2.
Death of the Fox by George Garrett

LIKE *AT THE MOON'S INN*, this work provides both an immensely valuable look at pre-Southern history and an introduction to a great Southern writer. George Garrett re-creates Elizabethan England in both broad scope and intimate detail. We must remember that this was the very world out of which the first settlers of Virginia and Carolina came and much of which they brought with them. And the central character is Sir Walter Ralegh, who never set foot in North America yet is one of the great figures of early American history.

George Palmer Garrett, Jr. (1929--2008) received considerable recognition during his career, but not as much as he merited. Like his great Southern forebears Poe and Simms and his contemporaries Fred Chappell and Wendell Berry, he was genuine "man of letters," excelling alike in fiction, poetry, and essays. And we can add screenwriting and the teaching of writing. Born and raised in old pre-Disney Florida, as a young man Garrett was a boxer and an Army noncom before going to Princeton and undertaking a literary career. He held professorships at a number of institutions, finally the University of Virginia. He wrote prolifically (on yellow legal pads) in multiple genres. Garrett was a humourous and unceasing critic of the phony literary pretensions of the cabal of Manhattan celebrities who bill themselves as the greatest contemporary American writers. This may be seen in his books *The Sorrows of Fat City* and *My Silk Purse or Yours*, among many others. At the same time he was a generous mentor to young writers with genuine talent. In his work Garrett's viewpoint is what might be called that of a sincere but tough and realistic Christian. *Entered from the Sun* is a prequel and *The Succession* is a sequel to *Death of the Fox*.

3.
The History and Present State of Virginia (1705) by Robert Beverley

WE MAY CALL THIS the first Southern book and the first American book, because that amounts to the same thing. For a long time the South was America. Robert Beverley (c. 1667--1722) was born in Virginia and was proud of it. He wrote this very first book by an American on an American subject in loving defense of his native land. At a time when New Englanders were penning crabbed Puritan tracts that could have been written in Europe. From the same motives, Thomas Jefferson was to write his only book, *Notes on the State of Virginia*, three-quarters of a century later.

Beverley deals not only with the history of his country but with its flora, its fauna, its geography, its climate, its agriculture, its way of living, its labour, its customs and laws, and in a lively and attractive way. And also sympathetically with its earlier inhabitants, the Native Americans. This is a glimpse of the early South by which we understand why Southerners saw America as a garden of enjoyment to be developed by courage and hard work, while New Englanders saw themselves on an imperious moralistic "mission into the wilderness." Which were the truer Americans? If you want to immerse yourself in early Virginia more deeply, look into Captain John Smith's *The General Historie of Virginia, New-England, and the Summer Isles* (1624).

4.
Charleston: The Place and the People (1906) by Mrs. St. Julien Ravenel

THIS IS A LIVELY and charming account of Charleston from its beginnings to 1860. The most interesting parts, perhaps, are about the early years of Indian wars, pirates, and Revolutionary War defense and occupation. There is much else about architecture, religion, culture, great plantations and famous families.

Harriott Horry Rutledge married St. Julien Revenel, a Confederate scientist who played a significant role in the defense of Charleston. She was descended on both sides and married into great Low Country families. She had affection for and intimate knowledge of her subject but also candid realism about human beings. This book can safely be called "a delightful read."

5.
Carolina Chronicles by Inglis Fletcher

IN A SERIES OF TWELVE books Inglis Fletcher conveys a broad and historically sound picture of the early days of North Carolina, which are less known than the comparable periods of Virginia and South Carolina, but arguably just as interesting. Pick one, perhaps *Raleigh's Eden* or *Toil of the Brave*, and I'll bet my "Smile When You Say Dixie" poster that you will want to read some more. The books are, in chronological order of content, *Roanoke Hundred, Bennett's Welcome, Rogue's Harbor, Men of Albemarle, Lusty Wind for Carolina, Cormorant's Brood, Raleigh's Eden, The Wind in the Forest, The Scotswoman, Toil of the Brave, Wicked Lady, Queen's Gift.*

Inglis Fletcher (1879—1969) was born in Illinois and lived all over the world with her mining engineer husband, but she became vitally interested in and devoted a prolific writing career to the settlement and Revolutionary experience of the Albemarle Sound region, which was the seat of her maternal forebears. She spent her later years there, in Edenton.

6.
The First Gentlemen of Virginia: Intellectual Qualities of the Early Colonial Ruling Class
by Louis B. Wright

LOUIS B. WRIGHT WAS an outstanding American scholar of the English Renaissance and American colonial life. This led him naturally to an interest in the first generations of Virginians before the Revolution, the fathers of those great Virginians who played so central and indispensable a role in founding the United States. He describes their intellectual, cultural, and political life in ample detail. This is a tour de force of intellectual history focused on the South. (I will forgive you if, after the first few times, you skip over the lists of books that made up an early Virginia planter's ample library.) After Wright nobody can honestly claim that early Southerners were culturally backward. In fact, it may be creditably argued that they were superior to their Northern counterparts. (If you want to explore the life of early Virginians further, get the several diaries of William Byrd II, one of Wright's subjects, which have been discovered and printed.) If you are really persevering, you could study the 3 volumes of *Intellectual Life in the Colonial South* by Richard Beale Davis.

Louis Booker Wright (1899—1984) was born in rural South Carolina and educated at Wofford College; then, after service in World War I and a stint as a pilot in the pioneer airmail service, he got a Ph.D. at the University of North Carolina. Wright was an untiring explorer of original sources and a prolific and enjoyable writer. He also played a major role in the development of two of the most important primary research institutions of the United States—the Huntington Library in California and the Folger Shakespeare Library in Washington of which he was director. Good follow-up reading can be found in any of Wright's books, in particular *The Colonial Search for a Southern Eden*.

7.
The Revolutionary War "Romances" of William Gilmore Simms

THE WAR OF AMERICAN INDEPENDENCE was a stalemate in the North and was won in the South by Southerners. Probably no one has ever known as much about the Revolution in the South as William Gilmore Simms, the South's greatest 19th century writer after Edgar Allan Poe. Simms had a large collection of Revolutionary War manuscripts (destroyed during Sherman's celebrated "March") and interviewed many veterans and their close relatives. He was an able historian but believed that the glorious achievement of American liberty would be best remembered if cast into a series of novels which he called "romances." These are *Joscelyn, The*

Partisan, Mellichampe, Katherine Walton, The Scout, The Forayers, Eutaw, and *Woodcraft. Woodcraft* is preferred by many readers because of its entertaining picture of Captain Porgy, a Falstaffian figure, as he adjusts to postwar life. *The Scout* and *The Partisan* portray vividly the fighting, and *Katherine Walton* pictures the pain of divided loyalties.

Pick one and you will be eager to read the others. Simms' "romances" of the Revolution, along with his "romances" of the colonial South (like *The Yemassee* and *The Cassique of Kiawah*) and his stories of the frontier South (like *The Wigwam and the Cabin*) are a major triumph of American literature.

William Gilmore Simms (1806—1870) of South Carolina excelled as poet, novelist, short story writer, historian, literary critic, and essayist, and journal editor. Poe said that if Simms had enjoyed the self-promotion machine of New England writers his name would be a household word. Contrary to what is sometimes claimed, he was not just interested in the gentry. His works sympathetically portray yeomen, frontiersmen, Indians, and African Americans. Nor was his writing crippled by "romanticism," as has been alleged. In his time the New England savants indeed condemned him for being too realistic and earthy, not genteel enough. Then, when kitchen-sink realism became the vogue, he was condemned as being too romantic. There are many economic and political costs to the South in losing a war, as well described in Ronald and Donald Kennedys' classic *Punished with Poverty*. There are also serious cultural costs, one being that Simms is still not given proper place in the canon of great American writers.

8.
The Life of Francis Marion
by William Gilmore Simms

NO GUIDE TO SOUTHERN BOOKS can fail to call attention to *The Life of Francis Marion: The True Story of South Carolina's Swamp Fox.* In his life of the modest hero whose partisan genius was critical in driving the British army from the South and winning the Revolutionary War, Simms had access to materials that no longer exist, having been lost as a result of Sherman's great civilisational expedition. Especially the memoirs of Peter Horry, Marion's right-hand man and second-in-command. Marion is truly a figure deserving fame. A 2007 edition contains the definitive text and an introduction by Professor Sean R. Busick, the authority on Simms's historianship. If your interest in the War of Independence in the South is piqued, follow on with Simms's biography of Nathanael Greene and William Moultrie's *Memoirs of the American Revolution*.

9.
The Language of the American South
by Cleanth Brooks

THE "SOUTHERN ACCENT" HAS long been a major identifier of Southern origins, quite often to outsiders a signal of an ignorant and/or evil person. Experts will hasten to declare that there is more than one Southern accent, which is true. Nevertheless the various accents tend to congregate together as an identifier. There has been much discussion of how the Southern accent(s) came about. Cleanth Brooks, among the greatest American literary scholars of the 20th century, was interested in the subject because he believed it was related to the world-class achievements of Southern writers. Brooks's contribution to answering the question of origins is definitive and will be surprising to some.

Cleanth Brooks (1906--1994) was born in Kentucky and attended Vanderbilt University. He was too young to participate in *I'll Take My Stand* but contributed to the follow-up Agrarian work, *Who Owns America?* Brooks became professor at Louisiana State University where he, with Robert Penn Warren, founded *The Southern Review*, which gained international recognition. In an incident that is all too common in Southern universities, Brooks and Warren were driven out of LSU by a carpetbagger president from Wisconsin with a dubious doctorate in

"Education." They wanted to remain in the South, but had to accept offers from Yale where their careers prospered. Brooks became the premier authority on William Faulkner (see his *William Faulkner: Yoknapatawpha Country*, among other works). And also a leading American literary critic and teacher with *Understanding Poetry* and *Understanding Fiction*, which were long in use as college textbooks. Brooks was also an insightful Southern commentator on the state of America, as can be seen in his *Community, Religion, and Literature*.

10.
Thomas Jefferson's Letters, 1760 - 1826

IF THOMAS JEFFERSON had never drafted the Declaration of Independence or been President of the United States, he would still be of major, permanent, and international interest for the voluminous written record of his capacious, broad-ranging, and questing mind. Many of Jefferson's public writings are well-known. I suggest dipping into the thousands of letters he wrote during a long and productive life as the best way to get to know and appreciate the real Jefferson. Jefferson has been put to so many misleading uses that he is almost unrecognisable in our time. An immersion in his own words as himself will be a refreshing cure for many false interpretations.

Two early editions of Jefferson's letters and other writings are incomplete and imperfect but accessible online: *The Writings of Thomas Jefferson*, edited by Paul L. Ford, 10 vols., and *The Writings of Thomas Jefferson*, edited by Lipscomb and Bergh, 20 volumes. Princeton University is slowly publishing a complete *Papers of Thomas Jefferson*, which may be viewed online for a fee. Two fairly available selected book editions are *The Life and Selected Writings of Thomas Jefferson*, edited by Adrienne Koch and William Peden, and *The Portable Thomas Jefferson*, edited by Merrill D. Peterson. These two more recent publications are a little light on Jefferson's states' rights and Southern views.

11.
A Better Guide Than Reason: Studies in the American Revolution by M.E. Bradford

M.E. BRADFORD'S INITIAL FIELD of scholarship was Southern and British literature. In his study of the Revolutionary era he mastered history and political thought as well, bringing all his learning together in a brilliant, original, and persuasive interpretation of the American Founding. A Northern commentator writes that "Bradford brings the founders alive for us intellectually" and that some of his essays are "among the most important of our time." Bradford's case is that the men who accomplished American independence and founded constitutional governments were NOT, contrary to later destructive interpretations, *philosophes* launching a permanent revolutionary movement for Equality. Rather, they were men grounded in the history of English law and liberty and soberly experienced in government, conservatives working to preserve the society they already had and were largely content with. The War of Independence was "not a revolution made, but a revolution averted."

Melvin E.A. Bradford (1934—1993) was a native of Oklahoma, received a Ph.D. at Vanderbilt University under the Agrarian Donald Davidson, and was for some years a professor at the University of Dallas. He was the prolific author of penetrating articles on many literary, cultural, and political subjects that won him a devoted following. An appreciation of Bradford's genius by nine well-known scholars is *A Defender of Southern Conservatism: M.E. Bradford and His Achievements*, edited by Clyde N. Wilson. To pursue further Bradford on the Founding, see his *Founding Fathers* (originally published as *A Worthy Company*), *Original Intentions: On the Making and Ratification of the United States Constitution*, and *Against the Barbarians and Other Reflections on Familiar Themes*.

12.
The Politically Incorrect Guide to the Founding Fathers by Brion McClanahan

THIS BOOK IS A TREASURE trove of neglected information about the Founders, and not just the more famous ones. It allows the reader to really see their true beliefs and motivations without the misleading interpretations put on their work by later purveyors of various agendas. McClanahan's readable, information-rich book provides massive evidence that coincides with Bradford's view described above. Both Bradford and McClanahan, it should be said, are just as knowledgeable about and sympathetic to the Northern Founders as they are to the Southern.

13.
Daniel Boone, Master of the Wilderness by John Bakeless

THIS IS IN MY OPINION the best, most complete, accurate, and understanding of the many biographies of the great Southern pioneer. It provides a true picture of the epic settlement of the Trans-Appalachian South.

John Bakeless (1894—1978) was a Pennsylvanian and a prolific author of books on the American frontier and the

American Revolution. He was a solid, old-fashioned historian who investigated thoroughly and told the story clearly with a minimum of personal opinion. There is a more recent biography of Boone by Robert Morgan, who is considered by some to be a notable Southern writer. Morgan's biography is too presentistic and makes too many sweeping generalizations. For instance, he can't tell the difference between Daniel Boone and Henry David Thoreau as representatives of the West. They would have despised each other. Thoreau never ventured out of sight of the Boston smokestacks and Boone is on record that he never met a Yankee he could trust.

14.
An Inquiry into the Principles and Policy of the Government of the United States (1814) by John Taylor of Caroline

JOHN TAYLOR (1753—1824) of Caroline County, Virginia, is the philosopher of the Jeffersonian republicanism that was long the basis of Southern social, political, and economic thought. To the principles that Jefferson represented in the public mind and that John Randolph of Roanoke dramatized in the halls of Congress, Taylor gave systematic exposition. He has been called one of the few political thinkers whose work is an original American contribution to political science. He was so highly regarded in his time that, though he never sought political office, he was twice appointed by Virginia to unexpired terms in the U.S. Senate. Jefferson said that he agreed with every word that Taylor wrote. Taylor represented at the same time a very Southern combination of conservative allegiance to local community and inherited ways and a radical-populist suspicion of government, "progress," and capitalist machinations. His works are critiques of the Federalist acts in the early days of the federal government that had betrayed the Revolution and destroyed the Constitution in order to profit a Northern mercenary elite that he called "the paper aristocracy." Northern conservatism, as expressed by John Adams and others, argued that majorities are untrustworthy. The people would soon learn to vote themselves the wealth of their betters—therefore a strong President and federal courts were needed with numerous "checks and balances" on majority action. Taylor turned this on its head in his *Inquiry*. The people were no danger. They went quietly about their business, producing the wealth of the country. The danger, through history, had always been a conniving minority who worked out plausible schemes to use the government to profit themselves while producing nothing. His case is compelling.

15.
Construction Construed and Constitutions Vindicated (1820) by John Taylor of Caroline

JOHN TAYLOR'S WORKS have often been accused of being difficult reading. His friend and ally Randolph of Roanoke is reported to have said that Taylor's books would do much good—if they could only be translated into English. The criticism is exaggerated. Once you get the hang of it, Taylor's prose is quite enjoyable and full of humour. He was not a school teacher expounding a subject but wrote in the style of an 18th century English gentleman essayist. You must think of him as a sagacious farmer talking to his neighbours on the portico after supper. He builds his case with indirection and in storytelling style—and what could be more Southern than that? In *Construction Construed* he takes on the Federalist distortions that had started destroying the real Constituion almost from the start. How mere verbiage like "necessary and proper" had deceitfully justified substantive powers that had never been granted. Once more, his case is convincing. In a just world, aspiring lawyers would be reading Taylor and not John Marshall. If you are a Taylor fan, as I am, you will want to look into his *Tyranny Unmasked* and *New Views of the Constitution*.

16.
The Great Meadow
by Elizabeth Madox Roberts

THE WORKS OF KENTUCKIAN Elizabeth Madox Roberts (1881—1941) are not unknown but are not as well-known and well-read as they should be. In her novels of various phases of Southern life, often about the plain folk, Roberts is a literary genius of what has been called "poetic realism." Her stories are down-to-earth but at the same time tell of human experiences that move the heart. "The Great Meadow" is Kentucky. The story is of pioneers on that new frontier during 1774—1781 and told from a woman's viewpoint.

17.
Andrew Jackson, Border Captain
by Marquis James

MARQUIS JAMES (1891—1955), an Oklahoman, was a well-known writer of the earlier 20th century and a Pulitzer Prize winner. Here he tells the story of Andrew Jackson's life up until 1824 when he became a presidential candidate. We see Jackson as a product of tough Scots-Irish pioneers, as a boy soldier in the War of Independence, as an adventurous early settler in

Tennessee, as the heroic leader of frontiersmen to victory over Indians and redcoats, as a Southern planter at home.

James's account of Jackson's life until the age of 43 is important in understanding who he was and his role in American history. The meaning of "Jacksonian Democracy" has been badly distorted by establishment historians like Arthur M. Schlesinger Jr. and Robert Remini, who have tried to take him out of the South and assimilate him to Northeastern liberalism. James also wrote *The Raven: A Biography of Sam Houston* which is good company for *Andrew Jackson, Border Captain*.

18.
John James Audubon: Writings and Drawings
(Modern Library)

AUDUBON IS JUSTLY FAMOUS for his extraordinary life as a wilderness traveler, painter, and recorder of American birdlife. He was also a fine writer who kept extensive journals that are a great source of information on American life of the time. There are many partial and selective publications of his diaries and other works. Perhaps the publication cited here is a good place to start.

John James Audubon (1785—1851) was born into a planter family in the French West Indies. He lived at times in Philadelphia and New York but most of his four decades of active work was done in the South, where he lived for long periods and was completely at home and *simpatico*. Those who love Audubon should also be interested in another scientific traveler in the Southern wilds from an earlier period: William Bartram, *Travels Through North and South Carolina, Georgia, East and West Florida, the Cherokee Country . . .*, published in 1791. Bartram was not interested in birds but in plants and soils and the Native Americans.

19.
Nullification, A Constitutional History, 1776 - 1833, 2 vols., by W. Kirk Wood

SOUTHERNERS LONG BELIEVED and acted upon the knowledge that the federal government was the limited agent of a confederation of the peoples of the several States as sovereign political communities. Conventional wisdom says that this belief was merely a made-up "compact theory" standing in the way of national greatness. Actually the compact idea is not a theory but a fact. It was the centralists who had to invent an emotional case about a sacred and eternal government somehow mystically created by the people as an amorphous mass. Walter Kirk Wood was professor of history at Alabama State University. He has made the most exhaustive search that has ever been made of the documentary evidence for State rights. He begins with an intense study of the constitutional record before the Revolution and takes it through two generations after the Founding. The work is part Wood's close reasoning from the evidence and part massive presentation of the documentary evidence itself, much of its previously neglected. Convincing truth about "original intentions" to anybody who really wants to know.

20.
The Life of John Randolph of Roanoke (1851) by Hugh A. Garland

NO SOUTHERN READING LIST can ignore Randolph of Roanoke, one of the most colorful and eloquent public figures in American history as well as a staunch representative of the South. A great quality of this old-fashioned work is the copious quotation from Randolph's incomparable letters and speeches. The reader gets to know Randolph very well. The author, Hugh A. Garland (1805—1854) was a Virginian and a well-known writer in behalf of the Democratic party in his time. Russell Kirk's biography of Randolph is also a good place to go.

21.
Essays and Reviews
by Edgar Allan Poe

POE, IN MY ALWAYS HUMBLE OPINION, was the greatest American writer of the 19th century, although the Northeastern literary establishment ignored or minimized him until European critics forced him to attention in the early 20th century. In his short life (1809—1849) Poe was a complete man-of-letters, outstanding in poetry, fiction, and essays. He invented the detective story and his horror tales have inspired countless bad movies. He is the greatest of American lyric poets to this day. He excelled equally as an essayist and critic of literature. Since his poetry and stories are familiar, I suggest that a reader who wants to know his writing better should look into his prose writings, which have been included in a Library of America edition listed above. My praise of Poe's essays will be found convincing by anyone who reads Poe on the nature of poetry, or his reviews of American writers of his time, designed to encourage an American (i.e., non-New England literature).

Although Poe was born incidentally in Boston and spent some years in New York, never let anyone tell you that he is not a Southern writer. Where outside the South can be found an America writer of such imagination? He very clearly, and even aggressively, considered himself

Southern. As a Southerner he waged literary war against the pretensions of New England, referring to the celebrated Yankee writers as "Frog-pondians"—big croakers in a little place that they mistook for the world.

22.
John C. Calhoun: American Portrait
by Margaret L. Coit

WHEN THIS BEAUTIFULLY-WRITTEN book received the Pulitzer Prize for Biography in 1951, it was generally agreed that Coit had redeemed Calhoun as a major and admirable, even heroic, figure in American history. One result was that a U.S. Senate committee chaired by John F. Kennedy selected Calhoun as one of the five greatest Senators of all time. How the times have changed! But Coit's book has not changed and is still a marvelous correction to presently-distorted history.

Margaret Louise Coit (1919—2003) grew up in Greensboro, North Carolina, and was educated at the Woman's College of North Carolina, now the University of North Carolina at Greensboro. She worked as a journalist in Washington before becoming a successful writer of a number of books, including a biography of Bernard Baruch, South Carolina-born adviser to Presidents. In later years she lived in Massachusetts with her farmer-poet husband Albert Elwell.

23.
Georgia Scenes (1835)
by A.B. Longstreet

GEORGIA SCENES: *Characters, Incidents, &c., in the First Half Century of the Republic* is considered a classic of early American literature. It portrays Georgia society colorfully in the period of its transition from rough frontier to a more settled condition. The author knew the time and society thoroughly from his experience riding the circuit as a Methodist minister. The work saw print originally as a series of anonymous humourous sketches by Longstreet in a newspaper he edited at Augusta, Georgia. The "scenes" alternate between the rough life of rural and small-town folk and portrayals, sometimes satirical, of those seeking greater gentility. The former are more interesting than the latter, as seen in such examples as "The Fight," "The Shooting Match," "The Militia Drill," and "The Horse-Swap."

Augustus Baldwin Longstreet (1790—1870) was not only a minister, a newspaper editor, and an author. He was also a lawyer, a judge, president of four Southern colleges, and a major defender of the South. (General James Longstreet was his nephew.)

[I cannot resist this story. Nine candidates for the 2004 Democratic presidential nomination were scheduled for a debate in Longstreet Theatre on the University of

South Carolina campus. The building is named for A.B. Longstreet, who had for a time been president of the college. It was a frequent venue for such events, including William F. Buckley's television shows. Then (gasp!) it was discovered that the site was named for a "defender of slavery." The event was moved a block over to Drayton Hall. Nobody noticed that the Drayton family had been large slaveholders.]

24.
New Orleans: The Place and the People (1895) by Grace King

GRACE ELIZABETH KING (1851—1932) was a lifelong resident of New Orleans and a successful and popular writer, probably best known for her fiction *Balcony Stories*. She writes of America's most unique city from its beginnings with insider knowledge and affection combined with historical scholarship that makes for a lively adventure for the reader. For historical scholarship King had the benefit of a long acquaintance with Charles E.A. Gayarre', the pioneer historian of French/Spanish Louisiana, and one of the less known but more important of American historians. And, of course, King wrote before the Politically Correct re-interpretation of Southern history. *Laissez les bon temps rouler!*

25.
The Essential Calhoun: Selections from Writings, Speeches, and Letters, edited by Clyde N. Wilson

IN MY TIME I HAVE BEEN GUILTY of perpetrating 40 or more books upon the innocent world. I regard *The Essential Calhoun* as the most important—the one for which I hope the longest life. I wrote in the Introduction: "John C. Calhoun was a major actor in the political history of nineteenth century America, whose dramatic career will always be of interest. However, he is equally important as a political thinker, in which he resembles the generation of the American Founding Fathers more than his own or later generations of statesmen. . . . This collection is designed to present a full-fledged Calhoun. . . . I hope the book . . . will establish Calhoun's importance on a broader basis." In the interest of the broader basis the book presents, besides the expected Constitutional discussions, Calhoun's prophetic wisdom in regard to war and foreign relations; his understanding of economic questions, superior that at of any other public man of the time; and his devotion to the "republican virtue" of the Founders—the character that allows a people to achieve and preserve liberty. A good recent work on Calhoun's thought is H. Lee Cheek, *Calhoun and Majority Rule,* a study of Calhoun's "A Disquisition on Government."

26.
The Carolina Housewife (1847)
by "a Lady of Charleston"

THIS CLASSIC COOKBOOK is not only a guide to forgotten delights of dining but is also a priceless picture of how our Southern forebears lived—at a time when every household had a big group around the table. The author was Sarah Rutledge, a Charlestonian who passed away in 1855. There is a nice facsimile edition with an introduction by a descendant of the author, Anna Wells Rutledge. Enjoy!

27.
The Coming of the Civil War
by Avery O. Craven

CRAVEN'S WORK WAS once considered a standard of American historiography for its lively, well-researched, and well-written account of how unreasonable and unrealistic people, North and South, brought on an unnecessary and frightfully destructive civil war. It has fallen out of favour because the Northern extremists he so well portrayed are now considered heroes bringing about a desirable destruction of the evil South. And because Craven's temperate and even-handed picture of antebellum Southern society, the best part of the book, is discounted. It remains a very readable account of the antebellum period, with much information that is now ignored.

Avery Odelle Craven (1885-1980) was born in Iowa, a descendant of Quaker abolitionists, entirely educated in the North, and received a Ph.D. from the University of Chicago where he was for many years Professor of History. He was thoroughly a Northerner, though accused of being a Southern apologist for his even-handedness. He did have a Southern connection—his wife was a daughter of the Georgia statesman Thomas E. Watson. All of Craven's works on the origins of the War between the States are worth reading. Of particular interest is his biography of the scientist and Southern patriot, *Edmund Ruffin, Southerner*.

28.
Adventures of Captain Simon Suggs (1845) by Johnson J. Hooper

JOHNSON JONES HOOPER (1815--1862) came from the tidewater South (Wilmington, North Carolina). Like so many others, Hooper moved west, to Alabama, to seek his fortune. For Hooper, as for other Southern authors, writing was a pastime, not an occupation. They wrote to amuse their neighbours and to make a record of their society at the moment in time when the frontier was becoming settled down. They had a good time and they were able to laugh at themselves. Unlike the New England scribblers (Emerson, Thoreau, Lowell, etc.) they did not set up to be intellectual gurus to dictate to society. Unlike New Englanders, they wrote stories of earthy realism and not ditties about sleigh rides to Grandma's house and imaginary Indians named Hiawatha. For a long time this literature of "Southwestern humourists" was considered unimportant, but it is now accepted as "the finest specimens of writing, overflowing with wit and sentiment. . . . permanent specimens of real American originality."

Captain Simon Suggs of the Tallapoosa County, Alabama, militia was very popular in his time, going through numerous editions. He is irrepressible, reprehensible, likable, and unforgettable. His favourite saying is "It is good to be shifty in a new country." Suggs's adventures begin when he is able to escape Georgia with some capital after beating his execrable father at cards—Simon can never resist a faro game. His subsequent escapades, cast satirically in the form of a campaign biography for a sheriff's election, are hilarious exercises in the shifts necessary to prosper in a "new country." The 1993 edition contains an essay on "Southwestern Humour" by Clyde N. Wilson.

29.
Slavery in the United States of America
by Louis Filler

LOUIS FILLER (1911—1998) was a versatile researcher and writer whose primary interest was in reform movements, having written a major study of abolitionists. Anyone interested in the African slavery that flourished in the U.S. from 1619 to 1865, and almost everyone is, can profit from the unique collection of documents made by Filler in *Slavery in the United States of America*. His stated purpose was to put the American institution in historical context, and he does so, engrossingly, with not a few surprises. Readers who want to make a more exhaustive study of slavery should turn to the classic *Roll, Jordan Roll: The World the Slaves Made* by Eugene Genovese. For the large free black population in the Old South see *Black Property Owners in the South, 1790—1915* by Loren Schweninger and *The Forgotten People: Cane River's Creoles* by Gary B. Mills. There is much material of interest in *The Slave Community* by John W. Blassingame. When it appeared in the early 20th century, the master historian Ulrich B. Phillips's *American Negro Slavery* was considered internationally as the pioneer classic on the subject. See also *Myths of American Slavery* by Walter D. Kennedy.

30.
The South in Northern Eyes, 1831—1861 by Howard R. Floan

FLOAN IN THIS 1958 WORK approaches his subject as a professor of literature, which he taught at Manhattan College. He examines the attitudes of a collection of Northern intellectuals toward the South. What emerges is a picture of people who, for their own reasons, came to regard the South with "repugnancy, anger, and fear." This book provides essential insight into the origins of the War Between the States. Interestingly, those writers who had first-hand knowledge of the South were much less hostile than those whose "South" existed only in their own minds. A good work along the same lines: Chester F. Dunham, *The Attitude of the Northern Clergy toward the South, 1860—1865.*

31.
The Great Plains by Walter Prescott Webb

THIS IS A CLASSIC STUDY, declared on its publication in 1931 to be an outstanding contribution to understanding the American West. Webb describes the adaptations that farming Southern civilization made as it moved across Texas into lands with an unfamiliar landscape and aridness. Webb (1888-1963), professor at the University of

Texas, is a lively and very readable historian. I recommend also his *Texas Rangers: A Century of Frontier Defense*. The Texas Rangers and their Colt .45s were an adaptation to the Great Plains need for mobile Indian fighting. Webb was attacked by Midwestern scholars who preferred sod-busters, farm machinery, and Yankee schoolmarms to his version of the plains. Webb was also the author of *Divided We Stand: The Crisis of a Frontierless Democracy*. It appeared in 1937, a few years after the Agrarian Manifesto *I'll Take My Stand* and in a similar theme attacked the economic exploitation of the South and West by Northern capitalists.

32.
The Wigwam and the Cabin (1856)
by William Gilmore Simms

SIMMS EXCELLED not only as a novelist but equally as an author of short stories. This collection contains tales exploring a wide variety of Southern experience, concentrating on the frontier and Native Americans. Not to downgrade James Fenimore Cooper, who deserves his fame, but Simms knew more about Indians, wrote more about Indians, and understood more about Indians than Cooper ever did. In all his writings he also has something Cooper lacked, a sense of humour. In this collection Simms's story, "Caloya, or the Loves of the Driver," is the first American story with an African-American main character. Poe, master of the mystery story, said that Simms's "Grayling" was the best such story ever. Other story collections: *The Writings of William Gilmore Simms: Stories and Tales* (1974), previously uncollected pieces, and *Tales of the South* (1996). His short stories show the Charlestonian Simms as a master of the tall tale of "Southwestern humour." See such stories as "Sharp Snaffles: How He Got His Capital and His Wife" and "Bald-Head Bill Bauldy." In the short novel *Paddy M'Gann, or the Demon of the Swamp*, a rugged South Carolina riverboat captain is by some freak of weather transmitted to New York City. His rollicking experiences allow Simms to satirise New York society and literary pretensions.

33.
Poetry and Essays of William Gilmore Simms

ONE CAN NEVER READ TOO MUCH Simms, if only in protest of the establishment "scholars" who continue to refuse him proper standing among the most important American writers of the 19th century. *Selected Poems of William Gilmore Simms*, edited by James E. Kibler, is a great work of scholarship. Simms's poetry is mostly not in book form but is scattered through numerous journals of the time, sometimes anonymously or pseudonymously. The first edition of this book was published in 1990. The expanded and revised edition of 2011 indicates that original Simms's works are still being discovered.

Not only Simms's quality but his productivity is astounding. A good introduction to his essays on historical and literary subjects is *Views and Reviews: In American History and Literature* (1846). Other outstanding short nonfiction writings will have to be sought out individually: "Poetry and the Practical," "The Social Principle," "The Sense of the Beautiful," and "South Carolina in the Revolution—the Social Moral." Fortunately, familiarity with all of Simms's known writings has been made possible by The Simms Initiative, which has put everything online. Several able and devoted scholars have been laboring for several decades now, with some success, to raise Simms's standing. Alas, his rise in stature has also attracted trivial professors of literature looking for something on which they can hang the latest trendy theories.

34.
The Plain Folk of the Old South (1949)
by Frank L. Owsley

IN THIS CLASSIC OWSLEY demonstrates that the Old South prior to the War Between the States, contrary to abolitionist and Republican propaganda, was not a backward oligarchy governed by a few rich planters. Rather it was a society with widespread property ownership and prosperity, governed by a vigorous white man's democracy as much or more so than was the North. It has often been stated that Owsley has been refuted, but that is not true. In fact, the more recent and thorough studies of antebellum Southern society bear him out. Owsley's thesis is important because if he is correct that the Confederacy was a consensual creation of the Southern people, then the war waged against it looks a lot less glorious. Owsley (1890—1956) was the historian among the Twelve Southerners of *I'll Take My Stand* and his original research was innovative and exhaustive. A collection of his articles, published as *Frank Lawrence Owsley: Historian of the Old South*, is also of interest.

35.
Lone Star: A History of Texas and the Texans by T.R. Fehrenbach

SOME NEWLY ENLIGHTENED secessionists on the Pacific Coast, frightened by the 2016 election, have been heard to say that "California is not a State, it is a country." Perhaps so, but the statement is vastly more true of Texas, which indeed has been an independent country. Texas deserves a first-class historian to tell its epic story. Fortunately, it found the right man in its loyal and no-nonsense son T.R. Fehrenbach. This is a classic and enduring work.

36.
Carolina Sports by Land and Water (1846)
by William Elliott

WILLIAM ELLIOTT (1788—1863) of Beaufort District, South Carolina, was a planter with among the largest holdings in the South. He was well-educated, had many interests and activities, and was a prolific non-professional writer in several genres. Beginning in 1829, Elliott published many sketches of hunting and fishing. They appeared in various Southern and New York sporting journals. This collection has enjoyed a long popularity and has been reprinted frequently. Elliott's "Devil Fishing" is considered one of the best fishing stories ever written. In a self-satirical sketch, "A Business Day at Chee-ha," he describes his neglecting business by succumbing to a temptation to go deer-hunting. This is a valuable picture of the life of a Low Country planter. If you are so unfortunate as to be stuck with a recent edition, you may safely ignore the PC introduction by a carpetbagger celebrity. Needless to say, hunting is a major theme of Southern life at all times. Elliott's Upcountry South Carolina contemporary, General Maxcy Gregg, was also an avid hunter. His manuscript sporting journals have been edited by Suzanne Johnson and will be published by Shotwell. If you want to follow this subject into the 20th century, try the writings of Havilah Babcock

(1898—1964) in his *My Health is Better in November, Jaybirds Go to Hell on Friday,* and other books.

37.
The Rise and Fall of the Plantation South
by Raimondo Luraghi

RAIMONDO LURAGHI of the University of Genoa was one of the twentieth century's most important European students of the American era of the War Between the States. He wrote, among other works, a superb history of the Confederate Navy and a general work on the War that has not been translated into English. In the work in hand, he writes a graceful appreciation of the society of the Old South. To state a sophisticated case briefly, he finds antebellum Southerners to be, as is claimed by their defenders, admirably honourable and non-materialistic.

38.
Our Fathers' Fields: A Southern Story
by James E. Kibler

IN 1989 JAMES KIBLER bought a dilapidated plantation in his native Newberry County, South Carolina. He restored the original plants, both useful and ornamental and began hands-on farming. In the process he began to discover the history of the place and the Hardy family who had settled it in 1786 and called it Maybinton. The result was *Our Fathers' Fields*, a beautiful account of two hundred years of a Southern place and the agrarian family life on that place—life including both white and black. The book was an instant classic, praised by top-flight writers. Shelby Foote, for instance, wrote that Kibler's work "brings us home to who were are by showing us where we came from."

James Everett Kibler was a long-time professor at the University of Georgia and is a major figure in scholarship on Southern literature, particularly in regard to bringing to light the many merits of William Gilmore Simms. But remarkably for a noted scholar, Kibler is also a complete man-of-letters—an accomplished poet and novelist.

39.
Bloodstains: An Epic History of the Politics That Produced the American Civil War. Vol. 2: The Demagogues
by Howard Ray White

HOWARD RAY WHITE grew-up in a house in that had been used as a hospital during the Battle of Nashville. Bloodstains could be seen on the floorboards, which kindled his lasting interest in understanding the War Between the States. A scientist, White brings his training to bear in an exhaustive and well-organised study, filled with little known but telling facts. In Volume 1, *The Nation Builders*, he describes how Southerners created a new country, The United States. Volume 2, *The Demagogues*, covers how Northern fanatics and rent-seekers brought on a war of secession by seeking to control the United States in their own interests. Here we have a candid look at the dubious character and unrighteous motives of people like Thaddeus Stevens, Charles Sumner, and Abraham Lincoln, and at their role in the course of political events that ended in war. Any reader who peruses White's information-rich work will never again be able to look at the war as simply a tale of Northern righteousness and Southern evil. White gives equally original, exhaustive, and convincing treatment to the war in Volume 3: *The Bleeding*; and to "Reconstruction" in Volume 4: *The Struggle for Healing*. *Bloodstains* is a remarkable original work on the central events of American history.

40.

The Makers of the Sacred Harp
by David W. Steel and Richard H. Hulan

THIS EXEMPLARY scholarly work provides a full study of the creation and spread of the shape-note singing that played such a large part in the cultural and religious life of the Old and New South. The book is particularly notable for its treatment of the neglected major figure in this music, William ("Singing Billy") Walker of Spartanburg,

South Carolina. Walker is responsible, as you probably have never heard, for the controlling versions of "Amazing Grace" and many other treasured hymns. Here is a unique aspect of Southern life that needs to be noted by all students of Dixie.

41.
Sut Lovingood: Yarns Spun by a Nat'ral Born Durn'd Fool (1867) by George W. Harris

GEORGE WASHINGTON HARRIS (1814—1869) has been described as "an authentic comic genius" and "the most original and gifted of all the antebellum humorists." Mark Twain obviously took something from Harris and both William Faulkner and Flannery O'Connor specifically cited Harris as an influence. Harris was a Tennessee River steamboat captain and a part-time writer of tales that were collected in a book after they had appeared in various journals. Though born in the North and living in Unionist Knoxville, Harris was a Confederate through and through. His character "Sut" is a hell-raising Tennessee mountaineer whose foolishness and aggressiveness are always getting him into scrapes from which he can survive only by flourishing a pistol or rapidly deploying his long legs for escape. "Simon Suggs" is a "good ole boy" but Sut is a much tougher customer, perhaps reflecting the hardening of Southern attitudes under the relentless attacks of the late antebellum period. My favourite pieces include how Sut found himself on the train with an anxious Abe Lincoln on the way to his inauguration and became a confidante to Lincoln's schemes; and Sut's postwar meditation on the bad character of "The Puritan Yankee." The first book publication was the one cited above. More available is the publication a century later under the title *High Times and Hard Times: Sketches and Tales*.

42.

North Over South: Northern Nationalism and American History in the Antebellum Era
by Susan-Mary Grant

GRANT IS BRITISH HISTORIAN with no purpose to defend the Old South in this work published in 2000. However, her interest in the subject of the rise of nationalism in the 19th century led her to examine rather than take for granted American "nationalism" in the period. Exploring sources that have long been evident but unrecognised, she has documented a Northern version of American nationalism that came into being as antagonism to the "un-American" South. An interesting example of recent scholarship which has begun to recognize that the North needs to be explained as well as the South. A few other examples: Marc Egnal, *Clash of Extremes: The Economic Origins of the Civil War*; Harlow W. Sheidley, *Sectional Nationalism: Massachusetts Conservatives and the Transformation of America;* Anne Farrow et al., *Complicity: How the North Promoted, Prolonged. And Profited from Slavery;* Richard F. Bensel, *Yankee Leviathan;* Jim Downs, *Sick from Freedom: African-American Illness and Suffering During the Civil War and Reconstruction;* Kirkpatrick Sale, *Emancipation Hell* (which is conveniently available from Shotwell Publishing). And perhaps the most interesting and useful: Thomas Fleming, *A Disease of the Public Mind.* In an earlier brilliant study, *Alternative Americas,* Anne W. Norton anticipated much of Grant's argument.

43.

A Lamb in His Bosom by Caroline Miller

THIS IS THE MOVING STORY of a woman's life in the newly settled region of South Georgia in the period before and during the War for Southern Independence. I read it more than 20 years ago and many of the scenes of the life of Southern people of that time and place are still fresh in my memory. This work by Caroline Miller (1903—1992), a Georgia native, won the Pulitzer Prize for fiction in 1933 but is not nearly as well-known as it should be.

44.
The Children of Pride: A True Story of Georgia and the Civil War, edited by Robert M. Myers

HERE ARE PRESENTED the intimate family letters of the admirable and distinguished Charles Colcock Jones family from 1845—1868. A good access to the love, honour and courage of the Southern civilization that was destroyed by war and invasion. **Warning:** The original 1972 publication of this book is a large reading commitment. However, by all means avoid the 1987 abridgment, which seems to have been deliberately designed to censor out everything good and create a Politically Correct version.

45.
Notes on Spain and the Spaniards in the Summer of 1859, With a Glance at Sardinia "by a Carolinian" [James Johnston Pettigrew]

JAMES JOHNSTON PETTIGREW (1828—1863) was born into an Eastern North Carolina plantation family, graduated first in his class at the University of North Carolina, studied at Berlin University, and was generally regarded as a "genius" by those who knew him. He was an active citizen of Charleston in the decade before the War Between the States and a highly-regarded Confederate officer who was mortally wounded at the age of 35 in the Gettysburg campaign, in which he played a conspicuous part. In two different sojourns, Pettigrew spent more than two years in Europe, especially attracted to Spain and Italy. He had this book privately printed in Charleston in 1861 before leaving for the army. It has been almost unknown, but those who read it judged it to be the work of an admirable writer and thinker, who cast his cultural observations in the form of an entertaining personal adventure Fortunately, the University of South Carolina Press re-published the book in 2010. It is a wonderful exhibit of the intellectual quality and liberal (in the original sense of the word) spirit that characterized the Old South culture, the potential of which was so cruelly truncated.

46.
Jefferson Davis, Unconquerable Heart
by Felicity Allen

MRS. ALLEN WORKED DEVOTEDLY for years on the research and writing of this marvelous biography of our first Confederate President. This exhaustive and sympathetic portrayal should be on every Southern bookshelf. Allen's work is so good that it has bumped off of our list Hudson Strode's excellent biography. Strode's first volume is *Jefferson Davis: American Patriot*, covering the period up to Davis's election as President of the Confederacy. Strode (1892—1976) was a Swedish-American born in Illinois. For 47 years he was a professor at the University of Alabama, noted for his creative writing courses and travel books. He began, he wrote, knowing nothing about Davis. When he looked into the record, he experienced an increasing admiration for the man and his life. Strode's Vol. 2 is *Jefferson Davis: Confederate President*, and Vol. 3 is *Jefferson Davis: Tragic Hero*.

47.
The Pursuit of Southern History: Presidential Addresses of the Southern Historical Association, 1935 - 1963, edited by George B. Tindall

THE SOUTHERN HISTORICAL ASSOCIATION was founded as a gathering of Southerners teaching and writing Southern history. The annual presidential address was an occasion for a mature and respected historian to deliver thoughtful comments on some aspect of the Southern past. This collection is rich in the knowledge, beliefs, and judgments of Southern historians of an earlier time, learned and professionally devoted to impartial history. The content will make a startling contrast for any reader who is used to the current output of the Southern Historical Association, when South-hating and Politically Correct "mainstream experts" have taken over Southern history.

48.
North Against South: The American Iliad, 1848 - 1877 by Ludwell H. Johnson

THIS IS A BOOK that should be read and re-read and digested by every American who wants to understand the causes, conduct, and results of the War Between the States. Most of the writing and general public knowledge of the central event in American history rests upon a Northern viewpoint—the South is to be understood as provoking war by resistance to a benevolent government in unforgivable defense of slavery. Written with strict professional historianship and superb mastery of the sources and literature, *North Against South* tells a different story—not by defending the South but by close examination of the motives and actions of the North. Ludwell Johnson was a Virginian with a Ph.D. from Johns Hopkins University and a long-time popular professor of history at William and Mary College. The book originally appeared under the title *Division and Reunion: America, 1844—1877*. Besides this book, Johnson left excellent articles scattered through many publications which urgently need to be gathered and published: "The

Plundering Generation" (on Republicans in the War era), on Lincoln mythology, on Lee's critics, on Ken Burns' television atrocity, and an interesting article about how the U.S. Supreme Court in postwar litigation was forced to admit that the Confederacy had been a legitimate government.

49.
The Politics of Dissolution: The Quest for a National Identity and the American Civil War, edited by Marshall L. DeRosa

IN THE WINTER OF 1860—1861, the people of seven Southern States voted to dissolve their connection with the Union which their fathers and grandfathers had founded. The Union was no longer a benefit but was a source of vulnerability to hatred, terrorism, and economic exploitation. Southern members of Congress honourably withdrew since their States were no longer in the Union. On departing they made speeches giving a friendly farewell to their colleagues, explaining the actions of their States, and expressing a wish that their peaceful and open exercise of the right of self-government would be accepted without violence. Professor Marshall DeRosa, best-known perhaps as the expert on the Confederate States Constitution, has illuminated this critical moment in history by collecting the speeches of the time. Southerners' sober and temperate farewells to the Union makes a good place to end our search for understanding of the Old South.

50. *Make your own selection*

. . . and let me know your choice at shotwell@sc.rr.com. I am sure I will have missed somebody's favourites.

And a Few More

A GOOD GENERAL WORK covering all periods is *A History of the South* by Francis B. Simkins and Charles P. Roland. Both authors are very good and independent-minded historians.

There are two works I must mention that are not much suited to leisure reading but are essential to anyone who wants to know Southern history.

1) *A History of Agriculture in the Southern United States to 1860* by Lewis Cecil Gray. Agriculture was the life of the South for over three centuries. Gray was an economist for the U.S. Department of Agriculture who prepared this truly expert, exhaustive, and well-presented work. Here is everything you could possibly want to know about the subject—lands, climates, crops, methods, markets, labour, large and small farmers.

2) *The South in American Literature, 1607—1900* by Jay B. Hubbell. Professor Hubbell of Duke University pioneered the research of Southern literature as an academic subject. In the process he demonstrated that the South had a long and strong literary tradition and brought to light many unjustly neglected writers.

Two old-fashioned series that are being discarded or shredded by the culture police and their obedient bureaucrat "librarians" contain a vast amount of useful information. Both are available online and on the used book market: *Library of Southern Literature*, 16 vols., 1906—1913, edited by Edward A. Alderman, Joel Chandler Harris et al.; *The South in the Building of the Nation*, 13 vols., 1909—1913, edited by Walter L. Fleming et al.

State histories are very important to students of the South but usually cover a period larger than that of this guide. Some suggestions, old and new: *Georgia: A Short History* by E. Merton Coulter; *Arkansas* by John Gould Fletcher; *History of Louisiana* by Charles E.A. Gayarre'; *History of South Carolina* by Edward McCrady; *North Carolina: A History* by William S. Powell; *History of Maryland* by Thomas J. Scharf.

A forgotten treasure of lost regional knowledge can be found in *The Rivers of America* series, 63 titles published between 1937 and 1974. All but a few of the rivers whose stories are told are Southern, including Donald Davidson's *The Tennessee*.

Due deference to my betters, prevents the author from listing his own work among the top fifty. But Southern readers may find something of interest in my *From Union to Empire, Defending Dixie,* and *The Yankee Problem.* The last mentioned is conveniently available from Shotwell Publishing.

About the Author

DR. CLYDE N. WILSON is Emeritus Distinguished Professor of History of the University of South Carolina, where he served from 1971 to 2006. He holds a Ph.D. from the University of North Carolina at Chapel Hill. Wilson was editor of the 28-volume edition of *The Papers of John C. Calhoun* which has received high praise. He is author or editor of more than 20 other books and over 700 articles, essays, and reviews in a variety of books and journals, and has lectured all over the U.S. and in Europe.

Dr. Wilson directed 17 doctoral dissertations, a number of which have been published. Books written or edited include *Why the South Will Survive*, *Carolina Cavalier: The Life and Mind of James Johnston Pettigrew*, *The Essential Calhoun*, three volumes of *The Dictionary of Literary Biography* on American Historians, *From Union to Empire: Essays in the Jeffersonian Tradition*, *Defending Dixie: Essays in Southern History and Culture*, *Chronicles of the South*, and *The Yankee Problem*.

Dr. Wilson is founding director of the Society of Independent Southern Historians; former president of the St. George Tucker Society for Southern Studies; recipient of the Bostick Prize for Contributions to South Carolina Letters, the first annual John Randolph Society Lifetime Achievement Award, and of the Robert E. Lee Medal of the Sons of Confederate Veterans. He is M.E.

Bradford Distinguished Professor of the Abbeville Institute; Contributing Editor of *Chronicles: A Magazine of American Culture*; founding dean of the Stephen D. Lee Institute, educational arm of the Sons of Confederate Veterans; and co-founder of Shotwell Publishing.

Dr. Wilson has two grown daughters, an excellent son-in-law, and two outstanding grandsons. He lives in the Dutch Fork of South Carolina, not far from the Santee Swamp where Francis Marion and his men rested between raids on the first invader.

Available from Shotwell Publishing

IF YOU ENJOYED THIS BOOK, perhaps some of our other titles will pique your interest. The following titles are currently available (or will be shortly) from Shotwell at Amazon and all major online book retailers.

SOUTHERN STUDIES

A Legion of Devils: Sherman in South Carolina by Karen Stokes

Annals of the Stupid Party: Republicans Before Trump by Clyde N. Wilson

Carolina Love Letters by Karen Stokes

Confederaphobia: An American Epidemic by Paul C. Graham

The Devil's Town: Hot Springs During the Gangster Era by Philip Leigh

Dismantling the Republic by Jerry C. Brewer

Dixie Rising: Rules for Rebels by James R. Kennedy

Emancipation Hell: The Tragedy Wrought By Lincoln's Emancipation Proclamation by Kirkpatrick Sale

From Founding Fathers to Fire Eaters: The Constitutional Doctrine of States' Rights in the Old South by James Routledge Roesch

Lies My Teacher Told Me: The True History of the War for Southern Independence by Clyde N. Wilson

Lincoln: As He Was by Dr. Charles T. Pace

Maryland, My Maryland: The Cultural Cleansing of a Small Southern State by Joyce Bennett.

Nullification: Reclaiming Consent of the Governed by Clyde N. Wilson

Punished with Poverty: The Suffering South by James R. & Walter D. Kennedy

Sacred Conviction: The South's Stand for Biblical by Jonathan Harris

Segregation: Federal Policy or Racism? by John Chodes

Southern Independence. Why War?- The War to Prevent Southern Independence by Dr. Charles T. Pace

Southerner, Take Your Stand! by John Vinson

Washington's KKK: The Union League During Southern Reconstruction by John Chodes.

When the Yankees Come: Former South Carolina Slaves Remember Sherman's Invasion. Edited with Introduction by Paul C. Graham

The Yankee Problem: An American Dilemma by Clyde N. Wilson

FICTION

GREEN ALTAR BOOKS (Literary Imprint)

A New England Romance & Other SOUTHERN Stories by Randall Ivey

Tiller by James Everett Kibler

GOLD-BUG MYSTERIES (Mystery & Suspense Imprint)

Billie Jo by Michael Andrew Grissom

Splintered: A New Orleans Tale by Brandi Perry

To Jekyll and Hide by Martin L. Wilson

Free Book Offer

Sign-up for new release notification and receive a free downloadable edition of *Lies My Teacher Told Me: The True History of the War for Southern Independence* by Dr. Clyde N. Wilson by visiting FreeLiesBook.com or by texting the word "Dixie" to 345345. You can always unsubscribe and keep the book, so you've got nothing to lose!

SOUTHERN WITHOUT APOLOGY.

www.ingramcontent.com/pod-product-compliance
Lightning Source LLC
Chambersburg PA
CBHW071750040426
42446CB00012B/2508